A Practical Tool Guide For Prioritizing Your Life

Places, Spaces, and Times

Dr. Stacy D. Coward, ThD, LPC, RN

Copyright © 2024 by Dr. Stacy Coward, ThD, LPC, RN

ISBN: 978-1-77883-288-8 (Paperback)

All rights reserved. No part of this publication may be reproduced, distributed, or transmitted in any form or by any means, including photocopying, recording, or other electronic or mechanical methods, without the prior written permission of the publisher, except in the case brief quotations embodied in critical reviews and other noncommercial uses permitted by copyright law.

The views expressed in this book are solely those of the author and do not necessarily reflect the views of the publisher, and the publisher hereby disclaims any responsibility for them.

BookSide Press
877-741-8091
www.booksidepress.com
orders@booksidepress.com

To those with a heart that gives without looking for a return.

To those who are authentically concerned about other people and continue to take blows, criticism, and lack while giving to others.

To those who continue to love and give in spite because you are passionate about love, helping, and service toward others.

To those who meet and serve others daily without concern for themselves or the sacrifices they make for their family and loved ones.

Author's Note

This book is written for you to teach you the Art of Loving Yourself. It is a tool to assist you in identifying key concepts and self-awareness of how you are currently taking care of yourself and those you say you love and why you are doing what you are doing. This book aims to have a clear picture of where you are now and, by the end of the book, where you are trying to go. Many people say they love themselves, yet they are the last to eat, sleep, go home, or benefit from the love. Love first begins with you taking care of yourself. Take care of your emotions so your behavior will carry you in the right direction. This is not a self-love book, but a workbook that will help your words and your actions of love align themselves. This book will help you make your words, dreams, and actions align as you labor in love. This book is an Artwork for Love in Action.

Contents

Introduction	It's Your Life	vii
Chapter One	There Are No Mistakes	1
Chapter Two	You Are on the Clock	4
Chapter Three	The Right Plan	8
Chapter Four	The Right Reasons	12
Chapter Five	The Right People	18
Chapter Six	The Right Activities	23
Chapter Seven	The Right Conversation	28
Chapter Eight	The Right Thinking	34
Chapter Nine	The Right Intentional Movements	38
Chapter Ten	The Right Stuff to Get off Your Plate	44
Chapter Eleven	The Right Reason to Keep Going	52
Chapter Twelve	The Right Answers	56

Introduction

I am excited about the opportunity to develop this next series on the Art of Loving Yourself.

Have you ever felt you had given everything to everyone, and nothing was left for you at the end of your day?

We often prepare many tables for other people without considering that we, too, have value and need to be protected, loved, cared for, and even catered to just as much as the next person.

This is especially true if you have a core value of love, service, empathy, and selfless service. After you have completed this book, my goal is that you consider your life and your value. We will explore the why behind your actions of love, service, empathy, and authentic concern that moves you to activities and behaviors.

New belief pattern: *You are uniquely designed with all your unique experiences being an essential part of your life.*

This book will prompt you to have insightful moments to help you focus your actions to become intentional in your time, effort, and energy.

It will also help you explore your behaviors and actions while allowing you to create boundaries and limitations for others and yourself.

You are precious to the equation, and this book is written to help you understand your value and self-worth. You deserve so much more than you can gain in this lifetime.

This book is written to give you a concise road map to taking care of yourself first and being okay with you being a part of the benefits package of your life.

No matter where your story may have begun, all these experiences played a part in the creation of your unique qualities and your unique personality. You were handcrafted and developed from the beginning of time. Every experience that you encountered from the time of your conception has been uniquely designed for your life. All your good memories, bad memories, great adventures, horrible experiences, childhood drama, and teenage dreams of great expectations have all made you who you are today. You are a handmade creation; although things may seem unfair, it did not happen to you. It happened to you. Today consider a "thank you" in spite of. Our life product was designed specifically for the lifestyle you need to become the most excellent version of yourself.

Chapter One

There Are No Mistakes

On a scale from 1 to 10

Question: *Do you believe your life is a journey toward your great work?*

Success Principle: Trust the process for your life especially when times are tough, knowing that it is all a part of your journey. Every moment will be used for your good. There will be nothing lost and nothing wasted from your journey.

Scripture: *Proverbs 24:16 (NIV), "For though the righteous fall seven times, they rise again."*

Quote: *"There are no mistakes or failures, only lessons" (Anonymous).*

Dr. Stacy D. Coward, ThD, LPC, RN

Many people have gone through very traumatic things. Some of these things were out of their control; it happened long before they could protect themselves. Understandably, you are angry, depressed, anxious, and negative when issues are not resolved. Whatever your story may have been today, I want you to know there are no mistakes. As difficult as that may be to believe, you are loved, cared for, and on your way toward your new life today. Embracing your past experiences can be a challenge because some of this was unfair to you. I agree with you. It was unfair, but it has been an intricate part of creating who you are today. Those experiences have become the fabric of your personality, lifestyle, thinking, protective factors, work ethic, motivation, perseverance, and all the other positive behaviors that serve you today resulting from what happened to you in your past. If you can give yourself permission to embrace your past experiences with the idea that there are no mistakes, you can allow yourself to grow from your past pain.

Pain points can be used to fortify you in the future. *"You were built explicitly for your journey."* Many of you have endured challenging circumstances. I am confident that some of your stories have created a weight on your shoulders that often leaves you feeling heavy because you have not dealt with all your past pain points. I want to encourage you today with the idea of knowing that you are still here because you were able to go through the journey, and you are still standing because, from the beginning of time, you were born, equipped, and ready to handle the amount of weight you have carried all these years today give yourself permission to no longer eat up your time note with taking past pain points. Give yourself permission to glean from those experiences what you need and challenge yourself to live in the present and prepare for your future.

We all were created with a purpose in mind. All the things that have occurred in our lives are pointers toward getting us in the direction we need to move. When you think about all the people who did not make it past their teens and early years, the fact that you have made it here clothed in your right mind and body speaks volumes about what is still awaiting you. Great work lives inside you; it is resting and waiting on you to ignite it with your mouth, hands, feet, energy, faith, strength, perseverance, and will move forward.

Many of the components of our past experiences have created the infrastructure for the road map to the journeys that lie ahead of us.

Save your time trying to improve other people's quality of life before you fix your quality of life. In other words, *"Deal with YOURSELF BEFORE you try to help someone else."*

Do you understand what makes you mad, sad, glad, or afraid? What are some of the things that trigger you, and have you wrapped up spending time in the wrong places with bad people?

Many people spend so much time working on other people's projects and problems that they cannot even begin to look at themselves. You don't want to face yourself because you don't want to deal with yourself. All these unresolved issues are sitting on the table, and it's easier for you to focus on other people's problems than your own. Today I want you to hold yourself accountable in dealing with your pressing issues, past traumas, and future woes. Once you deal with those parts, go back and celebrate your past accomplishments, sit in your present moments, and encourage yourself about your future experiences.

Chapter Two

You Are on the Clock

On a scale from 1 to 10

Question: *Where are you trying to go with the time cycle you have been given?*

Success Principle: Every moment is an opportunity for you to move closer toward the greatest version of yourself. Use your past experiences as a reminder of where you have come from and what you have learned. Use your present moments to prepare for your future life. Actively participate in the present day to enjoy every moment of your time cycle.

Scripture: *Ecclesiastes 3:1 (MSG), "There's an opportune time to do things, a right time for everything on the earth."*

Quote: *"Time is free, but it's priceless"* (Harvey Mackey).

A TIME NOTE, MUCH LIKE A DOLLAR BILL WITH THE LETTER "T" IN THE MIDDLE, WHERE YOU WOULD NORMALLY SEE A FACE OF VALUE. IT IS OUR PARTICULAR ALLOTTED TIME.

EACH PERSON HAS A DIFFERENT TIME NOTE THAT MUST BE USED WISELY. EVERY SECOND COUNTS, AND WE ARE SPENDING OUR TIME ON NOTES. OUR TIME NOTES ARE ALWAYS IN USE WHETHER WE ARE ACTIVELY USING THEM.

WE ARE THE VARIABLE TO HOW MUCH GETS COMPLETED ON THAT TIME NOTE. WE ARE ALL WORKING THROUGH OUR JOURNEY OF LIFE BUT AT DIFFERENT SPEEDS. EVERY MINUTE THAT YOU SPEND COMES FROM YOUR TIME NOTE. IT IS LIKE MONEY; ONCE IT IS SPENT, YOU CANNOT GET IT BACK.

IT IS EXTREMELY IMPORTANT TO UNDERSTAND THE NEED FOR URGENCY, CONSISTENCY, AND READJUSTMENTS THAT MOVE YOU TOWARD AN INTENDED PURPOSE SO THAT YOU DO NOT WASTE YOUR TIME NOTE.

Dr. Stacy D. Coward, ThD, LPC, RN

As we begin this next section, take a few moments to consider where you are intentionally placing your energy and for what journey you intend to go on. Where is your arrival place, space, and time?

Every day we make an active decision to allocate something somewhere something: time, money, effort, energy, words, moments, emotions. We are constantly making allotment decisions, and the problem is we often use it on the wrong people, places, and times. You may find yourself staying in the wrong places too long or dealing with bad people you do not honor or serve purposefully for their journey or that you cannot pour yourself into as a service because they do not celebrate who you are.

Question: *What if I really enjoy doing things for other people and it makes me happy?*

You are a steward of your activity. Stewardship is essential in growth and development. It is a beautiful thing to be a person that loves, serves, and gives compassionately to other people's goals, needs, and desires. The question is the time right for you to give of yourself at this present moment, with this present group, under these present circumstances. Should your resources of time, effort, money, social capital, and other things be allocated right now? Be disciplined enough to hold your horses instead of getting in the race when it's not your turn.

What does your future look like?

Think about what your life will look like at the end of your journey period now, just consider one year from now. Are the activities that you are doing aligning themselves to get you to your product?

When you put your time in a particular space, does it yield you a particular outcome?

Take the time to consider what your future holds for you and your role in making these opportunities come forward. How ever you spend your time is what you will see manifest itself one year from now. *The goal is for you to get in front of your change. You can actively and intentionally get in front of your activities to move yourself into the direction you have envisioned for your life* (Coward, 2023). How are you using your opportunities to navigate your movement in a linear direction? The use of vision boards, power of your tongue, power of visualization, power of social capital and networks, power of experiences all create a momentum toward a particular direction in your life. Use your time living in the present as you consider your future the activity of your hands that are producing the outcomes you intentionally desire.

Now, imagine yourself ten years from now. Who are you, and what are you doing? What does your life look like? Who is with you, and why are they with you? Have you considered that every moment that you are giving away to someone, it is time that you are taking away from your timeline? Even though you may enjoy doing certain things or being around certain people, is that activity giving you what you need to move forward in your life? There is no right or wrong answer to this question; it is only what you decide has the most value for you.

Chapter Three

The Right Plan

On a scale from 1 to 10

Question: *Where do you give your energy permission to create on your behalf?*

Success Principle: We can give our energy permission to work on our behalf for our future. Give your energy permission to operate in your future, creating a plan, seeking out people, resources, and support.

Scripture: *Proverbs 16:9, "The heart of man plans his way, but the LORD establishes his steps."*

Quote: *"A goal without a plan is just a wish" (Antoine de Saint-Exupéry).*

Getting in the Right Places, Spaces, and Times

The first step is to take the time to think about your future and what it looks like in detail with color, noise, smells, texture, and even taste. Intentionality is essential to the process because your energy needs somewhere to focus. The more precise the picture you give it, the more intentional your energy, efforts, and activities can become in helping you accomplish the life you dream of for yourself. Every day it would help if you did intentional exercises. Each person should complete these exercises in a quiet, unrushed environment where you can sit to give your mind time to process your future ideas. "If you can see it in your mind, you can hold it in your hand" (Bob Proctor). You must see it in your mind before you ever get it to become a tangible substance.

You have done so much for so many other people. It is your turn to take care of yourself, and giving yourself the time you need to develop intentionally is okay. You are the most valuable part of the equation, and you must take care of yourself to continue to care for all the people assigned to your legacy roster. Many people will be affected by your decisions. Your time, effort, and energy are significant, so get into the right places, spaces, and times.

Creating your desired life involves envisioning your future and bringing it into the present through affirmations.

Here's an example of a life statement based on your description: "I am an educated and prosperous individual, blessed and highly favored. I am the proud owner of a beautiful home by the lake. This home is not just any home but a spacious four-bedroom haven where I raise my wonderful, talented, caring, thoughtful children. I am happily married, sharing my life with a partner who complements me. I proudly own a sleek Range Rover, symbolizing my hard work and success. Above all, I am a successful business owner, living on my own terms, making a difference in the world through my work. This is my reality, and I affirm it every day."

Reading your statement aloud daily can help you internalize and manifest these goals into reality.

The power of "I AM" statements lies in their ability to shape our subconscious mind, influencing our thoughts, our actions, and ultimately, our reality.

Do this exercise at least once a day for ten minutes. Read it aloud every day until you have memorized it.

Now that you know who will be in your life and what that life looks like, let's consider why this is important. The challenge for accomplishing your goal can often be the lack of understanding of why you are trying to achieve a goal. Your goals will be driven by your why. The why is the gasoline that drives your motivation even when you want to give up. It is essential, especially during high-stress times, to point to the why.

Why do I play the game like my life depends on it? Because it really does. My future life depends on my ability to keep my storyline pushing in the face of adversity, stress, anxiety, depression, and frustration. It is easy to make yourself happy when the days are sunny, money is in the bank, everyone is cooperating, the boss likes you, and you have all the support you need to become a success. We are planning for the days when everything goes wrong, a mad day has come, you have insufficient funds in your checking account, and nobody will pick up the phone to help you. This is what you will need.

As you plan for your future, consider breaking it down into twenty-four-hour increments. It's important to work toward your goals consistently. While living in the present moment, keep your endgame in mind. By doing so, you allow God to work out the details that may otherwise concern you. Focus on the problems that are solvable and make changes where you can. For the things you cannot change, navigate around them in a way that allows you to still achieve your overall goal. It can be a challenge to balance living in the present moment while striving toward your future. It's important to practice mindfulness and self-awareness to stay grounded and enjoy the journey. Remember, it's not just about reaching your destination, but also about the experiences and people you encounter along the way. Embrace the talks, dinners, laughter, smiles, smells, and moments that make up your journey.

Chapter Four

The Right Reasons

On a scale from 1 to 10

Question: *Who are you doing all of this for?*

Success Principle: Your reason must be bigger than you, food, or any other provision. We were built to be used. Create a vision that serves outside of your circle of need.

Scripture: *Act 13:36, "Now when David had served God's purpose in his own generation, he fell asleep."*

Quote: "ALWAYS DO WHAT IS RIGHT. It will gratify half of mankind and astound the other" (Mark Twain).

A Practical Tool Guide For Prioritizing Your Life

We often work for people other than ourselves, which is a selfless and noble practice. It is also an excellent way to consider your life as a purposeful tool to benefit others. As noble as those sound, it is hard work, especially when the people you are sacrificing for do not even understand what you are trying to do for them. They take all your efforts for granted. You barely get a thank you, and they most certainly do not understand the concept of a labor of love when they are on the receiving is by far extremely challenging to care for and love others unconditionally, and you work as hard as you do for the benefit of others as you are served the last cold plate of leftovers. The harsh reality of this story is that this is the life of many people who play to win for the team. Everyone on the team is not really for the team. Everyone may not contribute to the overall growth, security, and development of the group, and frankly, the same people you are investing in may not have the capacity to understand the magnitude of your sacrifice. If you know this, you can keep yourself focused. When you think you are operating for any of these reasons, you have already lost the battle. Your why must be much bigger than any of these places. Your why must be from a positive core value that you continue to build upon, fall on, push from, and work from. The core values will be the driving force when things get rough.

Here is the easy part to answer.

The people most individuals make sacrifices for to ensure they have a better life typically include their children, family members, or loved ones. The motivation behind these sacrifices often stems from love, care, and the desire to provide a better future for them.

There are various categories of people we give our time. They include the children that parents often sacrifice to provide them with better opportunities in life. This could consist of working extra hours to afford better education, giving up personal time for their children's activities, or even sacrificing their dreams so their children can achieve theirs.

Some people make sacrifices for their family members, such as siblings, parents, or extended family. This could help them through a difficult time, to support them financially, or to help them achieve their goals. People will even give up their time for loved ones, including friends, partners, or anyone else someone deeply cares about. People often make sacrifices for their loved ones to help them succeed or show their appreciation to everybody else. Some people sacrifice for the greater good, such as community, society, or humanity. This could be through charitable work, public service, or other forms of altruism. Pushing these people toward or across the finish line of success demonstrates love, care, and appreciation. It's a way of giving back for the sacrifices they may have made for you or ensuring they have a better life. This is all wonderful, but you have given your energy to someone at the end of your time. Make sure your movements are calculated and strategic to ensure the right group of people gets you.

Here is the hard part to answer.

These are all very personal and introspective questions that require self-reflection. Think about the people in your life and how they make you feel, whether they bring you joy, comfort, and happiness. Do you find this with a family member, a friend, a partner, or a mentor? You don't have to limit yourself to one domain of thinking. Give yourself permission to make sure you are around people who empower, love, and take care of you. As you reflect on your relationships and interactions with others, how can you get the most out of those relationships, and who can make the most significant impact in their lives? Do you have people who support you, make you feel valued, and care for your well-being?

"Are your activities of choice bringing you closer to your authentic self?" Consider what you do in your free time. Do these activities align with your values, passions, and goals? Do they make you feel fulfilled and authentic to yourself?

"How do you feel when you are accomplishing these things?" Reflect on your feelings when you achieve something. Do you feel proud, satisfied, and content? Or do you feel empty and unfulfilled?

Remember, these questions are meant to help you understand yourself better and find your purpose or "why" in life. It's okay if you don't have all the answers right away. Self-discovery is a journey that takes time.

Our fundamental values act as a personal guide, steering us through life's choices and actions. These values, developed during our childhood as part of our personality formation, often anchor our decisions and emotions. Consequently, they shape our outlook on the world and determine how we navigate it. Many factors may impact our choices, but our core values are an essential driver of our behavior.

IDENTIFY YOUR CORE VALUES

Your core values are what make you tick. They create the lenses from which you view the world and make you operate as you do. Your CORE VALUES drive your behaviors. They were created based on your life experiences. Your core values were being developed before you even understood who you were. You might identify with safety, respect, and protection if raised in fear, lack, and violence. You might identify with charity, hope, and love if you were raised with plenty, love, and stability. Neither one is right nor wrong. It is just how you were built. You must specify the core principles of your function to understand the reasoning behind your actions.

There are many stories in your life that you have experienced that have created these core values. Again, they are neither right nor wrong. It is just who you are, and that's okay. It is essential to know so you understand why you are operating the way you do. It is also vital for everyone that loves you to know where your behaviors are coming from.

Recognizing that our core values guide our actions, reactions, and behaviors is a significant step toward self-improvement.

Consider the importance of the need to align our actions with our values and goals and to become more self-aware of our responses, especially when they might lead us astray.

Have you ever wondered why you got so upset about something that did not match? When you think about all the things that make you glad, sad, mad, or afraid, where is it coming from? Why does it rub you that way? The very infrastructure of who you are is the framework from which all your decision-making activities occur. As you become more self-aware of your internal sensors, it's important to turn your emotions in the right direction. How can you use your emotions to help guide your behaviors so that time is not wasted?

Your commitment to pause and reflect before reacting is a powerful strategy for maintaining control over your actions and ensuring they align with your plans.

Are you able to breathe through your moments so that you can reset your thinking on the spot, in the moment when it is most needed?

During moments of self-awareness, it's crucial to have a reset calibrator for your emotions, which can be achieved through deep breathing exercises. By not being mindful of how you spend your time, especially when your emotions are running high, you risk wasting valuable opportunities. Don't let your emotions control your life in an aimless manner.

Chapter Five

The Right People

On a scale from 1 to 10

Question: *Who will benefit because of your time, effort, and energy?*

Success Principle: You GIVE yourself AWAY with every interaction therefore choose who gets you.

Scripture: *Proverbs 13:20, "Walk with the wise and become wise; associate with fools and get in trouble."*

Quote: "If you want to know who you are look at your closest friends, they are a mirror of who you are" (Dr. Stacy Coward).

Your presence holds immense value and has the power to change the dynamics of those around you. Your impact is evident in the way the atmosphere of a room changes when you enter it. Whether you believe it or not, your presence adds value to space. The question is, are you a positive or negative variable in the equation? Your actions should add value to the space. Your words should create an impact. Your time should yield a return. You should strive to make a difference in the spaces you inhabit. Every day, you make a deposit somewhere into someone or something. It's important to be intentional about the effort and energy you put into each space. When in doubt, take a moment to dream, think, and imagine a new future. Give yourself the time to become the greatest version of yourself. Deep breathing exercises and mindfulness meditation practices can help you hear what you're supposed to be doing at a particular season. Take a few moments now to imagine who you are becoming. See yourself dressed the way you like, with your hair exactly the way you want it. See yourself walking in your spaces, receiving awards, enjoying prosperity and good health. To become who you want to be, you must first see it. Take a few moments just to imagine your beautiful life.

Now consider the following questions to ensure you are giving your time to the right people.

WHO AND WHAT IS WASTING YOUR TIME?

Now imagine it is your funeral, and they are reading off the story of your life. Will your account be one of triumph or tragedy? Will you leave a story of hope or hopelessness? Will you be remembered as a name and a dash between two dates? The harsh reality of this story is that many people have not even considered the possibility of their lives amounting to nothing tangible after they leave this earthly realm. No one will be affected if they go. No one will have a missing part of the equation because they have spent their time in the wrong spaces and places, and ultimately, time caught them sleeping their life away. They are sleeping in the reality of the clock ticking and people waiting on them to arrive with the answers in life. They are sleeping on the need to be always fully operational. They are sleeping on being intentional and consistent with all of their movements, and by the time they wake up, the clock has stopped ticking, and their time is up.

TIME ASSESSMENT

If you are not seizing opportunities and moments and creating the scenarios you want for your life, you are losing ground and time in this life cycle.

This exercise will help you to determine who or what you are spending your life cycle of time on daily.

WHO ARE YOU TALKING ON THE PHONE TO EVERY DAY? HOW OFTEN AND HOW LONG IS THE AVERAGE CONVERSATION? DO YOU FEEL BETTER WHEN YOU HANG UP? WHAT GOAL DID YOU COMPLETE THIS WEEK?

Think about the activities that you are doing. Do they align with where you are going? All your goals should be directed toward the main goal. Write down three goals that you would like to have completed this week and make sure that they are in alignment with your overall success goal.

A Practical Tool Guide For Prioritizing Your Life

WHO TEXTED/CALLED YOU BEFORE 0900 THIS MORNING AND DO YOU WANT THEM TO HAVE THE ABILITY TO TEXT/CALL YOU BEFORE 0900?

Who deserves your complete attention before everyone else? Only those who hold a priority position in your life should be contacted before 9:00 a.m. Business hours run from 9:00 a.m. to 5:00 p.m., so it's important not to mix these two groups of people. The time between 4:00 a.m. and 9:00 a.m. should be reserved for activities that enrich your life and your inner circle. After work hours, you can focus on building and strengthening relationships with those people you have already established a desire to be with. Remember to separate your work and play hours so you can be productive in both areas.

WHO IS IN YOUR PHONE LOG THIS WEEK? IS EVERY PERSON ON THE LOG SOMEONE YOU WANT TO GIVE YOUR TIME TO? IF SO, NOT WHY?

Have you ever stopped to think about who you're spending your phone time talking to and why they have your undivided attention? With all the technological advancements at our disposal, we can communicate in a multitude of ways, from texting and emailing to video calling. But when we're on the phone, we're giving someone our complete focus for a certain period. It's crucial to carefully consider the individuals we choose to give our phone time to, as it detracts from our precious time.

Dr. Stacy D. Coward, ThD, LPC, RN

WHO TOLD YOU THEY LOVED YOU THIS WEEK? HOW DID THAT MAKE YOU FEEL?

Who have you spent time with this week and heard the words

"I love you" from? It is important that you keep a check on your inner circles and that you surround yourself around people so that at the end of the day you can hear the words you are loved, you are cared for, you are valued. If you do not have a circle of people around that these phrases freely flow through, then consider adding the right variations of people in your life so that you can hear the words "I love you" on a consistent basis.

WHO DID YOU KISS THIS WEEK?

Who are you closely related to that you can hug or kiss even if it's on the cheek? Maintaining intimate relationships helps to create love and belonging and allows you to feel connected to a particular group of people. Intimacy can be gained in so many ways that include hand-holding, hugs, forehead kisses, or even just sitting together. It is important to maintain a sense of intimacy with someone.

Chapter Six

The Right Activities

On a scale from 1 to 10

Question: *How much time are you spending on the right activities of CHOICE?*

Success Principle: Knowing exactly what you should be doing when you should be doing it is half of your time management solution.

Scripture: *Galatians 6:9, "Let us not lose heart in doing good, for in due time we will reap if we do not grow weary."*

Quote: "You CREATE your life with every decision you make, so choose wisely" (Dr. Stacy Coward).

Dr. Stacy D. Coward, ThD, LPC, RN

HOW MANY HOURS DID YOU WORK THIS WEEK FOR A PAID JOB?

It is important to put time in the places that create value for you. There is nothing wrong with working for money, but it is more important to work in places that yield you peace, love, fulfillment, legacy, self-value, and ultimately, self-actualization.

HOW MANY HOMECOOKED MEALS DID YOU EAT?

Have you made a meal for yourself this week and sat down with your family to have a meaningful conversation? Preparing meals is not just about satisfying your hunger; it is an opportunity to connect with your loved ones or even yourself. You can reflect on your day or discuss your future over a delicious meal. Don't underestimate the power of cooking and sharing a meal together. It is a valuable use of your time and a chance to bond with the people you cherish the most.

HOW MANY HOURS DID YOU WORK THIS WEEK ON THINGS YOU DID NOT GET PAID ON?

Keep a good work-life balance by working on things that you are not getting paid for that create intrinsic value for you and intrinsic reward. You must invest time in places that reward you spiritually and emotionally. If you are not putting time in these places, you are at a deficit in your life and it will quickly become unbalanced.

HOW MUCH TIME DID YOU SPEND IN SPIRITUAL PRACTICES?

Your spiritual practices are individualized. Whatever you choose to practice is your individual choice. If you are making an investment in that space and time to develop and grow a relationship as well as have spiritual maturity, it is about the relationship that you have with your higher power and how you lean into that higher power when you need strengthening.

HOW MUCH TIME DID YOU ACTUALLY SPEND WORKING WHILE AT WORK?

Are you actively working on the job you are being paid to work on, or do you spend time thinking in other spaces while you are being paid for a particular job? This is a clear indicator that you should consider relocating your body so that your mind and body and activity can all be present. Don't waste your valuable time sitting behind a desk that you do not value.

WHAT WERE YOU DOING WHILE YOU WERE NOT ACTIVELY WORKING?

If you are spending your time behind a desk thinking or doing other activities that do not have anything to do with your current workplace, this is an indication that you are in the wrong place with the wrong people at the wrong time. I know this can be difficult to move from this space because you are depending on it for income, stability, or familiarity. Trust yourself and challenge the belief that you cannot get a new job. What you are seeking

Dr. Stacy D. Coward, ThD, LPC, RN

is actively seeking you. Put yourself in a position where you can readjust and reestablish a new beginning for yourself. If you don't start today, it will never happen.

DID YOU SPEND MORE THAN 15 MINUTES OUTDOORS THIS WEEK AT ONE TIME?

Spending time in nature can help you realize how vast and wonderful the world is. Your life extends far beyond the confines of your workplace. By stepping outside, you can witness the beauty of the world and all the opportunities it holds. Whenever you feel stressed or overwhelmed, take a moment to appreciate the simplicity of nature—observe a tree, a bird, a cloud, or even an ant. Sometimes the most magnificent things are right in front of us, but we fail to notice them.

HOW MUCH TIME DID YOU SPEND ON PERSONAL GROOMING THIS WEEK?

It's important to take some time for yourself because you are the most important person in your life. Personal grooming is a way to show yourself some love and attention, and it's a clear sign that you're prioritizing your own needs. Many people spend all their time taking care of others, but it's important to remember that you deserve to be taken care of too. Treat yourself to a haircut, put on some makeup, wear clean clothes and new shoes. You are valuable and everyone else depends on you, so it's vital that you take care of yourself.

DID YOU SPEND ANY TIME EXERCISING YOUR BODY?

To ensure that your body functions at its best, it's important to give your heart, lungs, skin, kidneys, and liver the oxygen they need. Regular exercise helps your body operate at its full capacity. By dedicating 30 to 45 minutes to exercise two to three times per week, you demonstrate that you value your body and want to care for it. Taking care of yourself in this way enables your body to take care of you and helps you move through life.

Chapter Seven

The Right Conversation

On a scale from 1 to 10

Question: *How often do you use your tongue to bring you good gifts?*

Success Principle: Use your mouth to cosign on opportunities to bring resources, people, finances, and growth moments into your life.

Scripture: *Ephesians 4:29, "Let no unwholesome word proceed from your mouth, but only such a word as is good for edification according to the need of the moment, so that it will give grace to those who hear."*

Quote: "Don't let your words betray you" (Dr. Stacy Coward).

WHAT WAS YOUR MAIN TOPIC OF CONVERSATION THIS WEEK?

What are you spending your time talking about, and who is the main person of your storyline this week? Make sure that your mouth power is being used in a place that empowers you and empowers others around you. Don't waste your valuable time using your mouth in a way that does not edify you and others around you.

WHEN HAVE YOU LAST SPOKEN TO YOUR CLOSEST FRIENDS?

Your closest friends are the mirrors to your life; they remind you of who you are and why you live the way that you live. Remember we choose friends, not family. These people are your closest friends because they have been there for you when no one else was there and they also remind you of who you are and what you say you want to be in your life. Take time to lean into your closest friends on a consistent basis as a reminder of who you are and what you stand for.

Money talks, so if you want to know what's important to you and what you value the most, what did you spend your money on?

WHAT ARE YOU SPENDING YOUR MONEY ON WEEKLY? LOOK AT YOUR RECEIPTS, BANK STATEMENT, OR ELECTRONIC PAYMENTS SYSTEM FOR AN ACCURATE ANSWER.

It's a good idea to set aside some time this week to review and categorize your bank account transactions. How you spend your money reflects where your time and energy go, and for many people, time is money. When you spend your money, you're essentially giving away the time you spent earning it in the past few weeks. Every dollar you spend represents a chunk of your time and energy, so it's important to be mindful of how you choose to allocate your resources.

HOW MUCH MONEY DID YOU GIVE AWAY OUTSIDE OF YOUR IMMEDIATE HOUSEHOLD THIS MONTH?

Have you ever considered the amount of money you give to people outside of your immediate household? It's essential to think about why you're allocating your resources in this way. What's your goal for using your resources responsibly? And how can you be a careful steward of your time, energy, money, and expertise? It's crucial to use our resources wisely and avoid giving them away thoughtlessly. Before distributing your resources, consider whether they could be used to create a system that would prevent the problem from happening again. Remember that we have a duty to take care of the things that God has entrusted to us. How were you able to navigate your internal dialogue to help you to do the things that needed to be done for yourself? Do you feel like you have enough value to do the things that make you feel good on a consistent basis? Do you value yourself enough to make investments daily? Creating a happy list for yourself is an essential practice for managing your emotional well-being as you manage your timed activities.

DID YOU DO SOMETHING FOR YOURSELF THIS WEEK?

It's important to find something that brings you joy and happiness. Take at least 15 minutes each week to do something that has value to you. Make a list of 50 things that you enjoy doing that don't involve money and try to do three to five of those things every day. Once a week, spend at least an hour doing something from your list to recharge and rejuvenate yourself. Remember to prioritize self-care and doing things that make you happy.

HOW OFTEN THIS WEEK DID YOU MAKE A CONSCIOUS EFFORT TO TAKE CARE OF YOUR HEALTH AND WELLNESS?

When is the last time that you scheduled yourself an appointment with the doctor so that you could have a well check up to make sure that your body is working correctly? Annual checkups are important because your body is a machine that needs a tune-up every now and then. You won't know what you need unless someone looks at it. Get in the habit of having annual checkups and Wellness visits with your practitioner of choice.

HOW MANY PEOPLE THANKED YOU FOR YOUR HELP THIS WEEK? FOR WHAT?

Making investments in other people is important. You know that you have made investments in other people because you will hear the word "thank you." Be careful not to get caught up in other people's gratitude for the things that you do.

Dr. Stacy D. Coward, ThD, LPC, RN

Do what you do because it's what you do. Being told thank you is a wonderful idea, but knowing that you did a great job is even better.

WHO DID YOU CALL ON YOUR FREE TIME? DID YOU FEEL GOOD AFTERWARD?

During your free moments, who do you pick up the phone and say, "Hey, what are you doing?" Make sure that who you are giving yourself away to make you feel good when you hang up the phone. Don't waste your time calling people to pour out negativity, listen to gossip, reinforce things that hurt you and do not empower you. If you get my ear time, it must put something in me that will give me the strength to work through my day and become the greater version of myself. Who's in your ear really does matter.

WHO DID YOU EAT LUNCH AND DINNER WITH THIS WEEK? WAS IT PLEASURABLE?

Spending time sitting at a table with the people that you love the most is one of the best opportunities you could have to share yourself. Think about it when you're eating, you're open, vulnerable, taking in substance. That is the best time to hear what other people have to say that you love and give of yourself freely in an unconditional and loving space. Sitting at tables eating with people that you do not love nor value is one of the worst uses of your time because you can do a lot of things with people, but you don't have to break bread. Use your moments of breaking bread with people that you value.

WHAT GOALS HAVE YOU BEEN TALKING ABOUT FOR AT LEAST THREE YEARS BUT HAVE NOT STARTED?

You have spent a lot of time talking about things, but there's no action to it. Why is there no fruit behind the labor of what you have put in? If you have put your time into a place and started it, then it is good enough for you to finish it. At least finish the project that you have started and allow it to stand up on its feet. When it is okay for you to dive into places that are unknown, sometimes it is scary when you don't know what to expect and it's safer to continue doing the things that you have done in the past. I understand that familiarity is comfortable. Being willing to explore things that you do not know about will stretch you into a new way of thinking, living, behaving, and knowing.

Chapter Eight

The Right Thinking

On a scale from 1 to 10

Question: *How often do you spend time thinking about moments that can strengthen you to turn your life in toward a positive direction?*

Success Principle: Direct your thinking by actively creating moments for thoughtful reflection and imagination that promote your growth and development.

Scripture: *Philippians 4:8, "Finally, brethren, whatsoever things are true, whatsoever things are honest, whatsoever things are just, whatsoever things are pure, whatsoever things are lovely, whatsoever things are of good report; if there be any virtue, and if there be any praise, think on these things."*

Quote: "Whatever you think gets into your heart; Whatever is on your heart gets on your tongue; Whatever you speak becomes a part of your life. Therefore, guard your thinking at all costs" (Dr. Stacy Coward).

A Practical Tool Guide For Prioritizing Your Life

WHO ARE YOU HOLDING HARSH FEELING FOR THAT IF THEY DIED TODAY, YOU WOULD REGRET IT?

Let go of any harsh feelings you have toward anyone, release it, and allow yourself to be released. If the person that you feel angry toward is living today and something happened to them, would you regret it because you did not fix a situation that you easily could have taken care of through an "I'm sorry"? Don't waste valuable time being upset with people about a past conversation.

HOW MANY PEOPLE DID YOU SAY "NO" TO THIS WEEK? WHY?

Say no and move on. Saying no allows you to preserve your energy for the groups that you want to spend time with as well as gives you an opportunity to be selective about who gets you. You are a valuable commodity and should not say yes to everybody and everything. Become particular about who you give yourself away to freely.

WHO DO YOU NEED TO FORGIVE SO YOU CAN MOVE ON?

Is there any person that is in your past that you have not forgiven? Unforgiveness holds you captive to a particular person. Forgiving them allows you to free yourself and move on to do bigger and better things. Sometimes it takes you to give up your right to be right to be free. Rest assured that no one gets away with anything that they have put out into the universe, but you holding on to the anger only holds you chained to them. Set yourself free by giving that person a pass for that offense. Move on and become great.

HOW MANY PEOPLE DID YOU COMMIT TO THIS WEEK? WHY ARE YOU COMMITTING TO THEM? DOES IT TAKE AWAY FROM THINGS YOU SHOULD BE DOING?

Stop making commitments to people haphazardly. Make sure that you have an out for your commitment as well as the criteria for how long you will commit to them. Commitment should not be indefinite between people; there should be a renegotiation of the terms of your commitment at least annually. This is not to say leave your spouse, job, agreements, etc., if you're not happy. It nearly says come back to the table and decide what the terms of the commitment look like.

HOW MANY TIMES HAVE YOU HAD INTIMATE RELATIONS THIS MONTH? WAS IT ENOUGH FOR YOU AND THEM?

The relationships that you have should yield you a sense of connection to a person. Intimacy can be done in many ways excluding actual intercourse; the goal is that you are creating intimate circles with people that you can be your authentic self around, and when you are in need, you have the social capital around you that creates resources for you to gain support during difficult times.

WHO DID YOU HUG THIS WEEK? IF NO ONE, THEN WHO SHOULD YOU HUG IN GRATITUDE AND AFFECTION?

There should be groups of people around you that you feel grateful enough to be around that a hug is merited. Who was in your circle that has created a sense of respect that when you greet them, it is with a hug, and when you leave them, it is with a hug. Gaining social networks that create a sense of value and respect is important to your growth and development.

WHO DID YOU THANK FOR HELPING YOU? IF NO ONE, THINK ABOUT SOMEONE THAT YOU CAN THANK FOR ANYTHING THEY MAY HAVE DONE FOR YOU.

Take the time to thank the people that are around you that are supporting you on your journey. Think about those people that are around you daily that work tirelessly to assist you in your life. Even if it's only one person that is around you that continues to be a support and framework to help you move your life to the next level, take the time to say, "Thank you for being there for me." You need them for your life, and they need to know how important they are in your life.

Chapter Nine

The Right Intentional Movements

On a scale from 1 to 10

Question: *How often do you intentionally make choices?*

Success Principle: Get in front of how you are using your hands and you will get in front of your movement.

Scripture: *Eph. 5:15–17, "Look carefully then how you walk, not as unwise but as wise, [16] making the best use of the time, because the days are evil. [17] Therefore do not be foolish, but understand what the will of the Lord is."*

Quote: "You have the power to intentionally change your life one step at a time."

INTENTIONALITY

It is important to become intentional about your movement, and activity is a key component to your success. Do not waste your time, money, resources, and energy in the wrong places, spaces, and times. It is time out for you feeding everyone and nothing is left over for you and the people who really matter the most to you. Don't get me wrong, service should go outside of your household, but to be effective, there must be a particular target group that gets a scheduled amount of time, energy, and resources.

WHO DID YOU HELP OUTSIDE OF YOUR IMMEDIATE FAMILY THIS WEEK? FOR HOW LONG? WHY DID YOU HAVE TO DO IT?

Taking time to help people outside of your immediate family and social circle is important, but also knowing how much time that you want to give to them as well as resources is important. Making investments in other people outside of your family certainly sows seeds that will ultimately return to your family. Just make sure that you are giving yourself away to a particular person or group that has meaning and will take your time and use it the right way. You give yourself away all the time; make sure that you pour yourself into a place where you can see the fruit of your labor yield itself.

NAME THE PLACES YOU DROVE YOUR CAR TO THIS WEEK.

Wherever you are driving your car to is where you are giving yourself away. There is a particular space that you need to decide gets you and your time. Driving your car to a person or place means that you value them enough to spend your gas, money, and time to be with them, making sure that you are driving your vehicle exactly where you want it to be for that time.

WHERE DID YOU SIT FROM 10 AM TO 4 PM? WERE YOU HAPPY THERE?

These are the normal work hours for most people; the question is, during these hours, were you happy? How do you feel when you're sitting in this space? Take some time and look around the space and ask yourself, is this where you want to be? If you dropped dead today, would this space be where you would say, "I was in a good place"? Don't waste another moment looking around at some dingy walls, in a dark room, around a group of people that you really don't like. The space that you operate from says everything about who you are. Is a space you're in clean, organized, and providing meaningful activity?

WHERE DID YOU LIE FROM 11 PM TO 4:30 AM? WERE YOU HAPPY THERE?

When you resolve your day, are you able to lie in a space that provides you comfort as a reward for your day? The end of the day should be a reward for all the hard work that you have put in for the day. Take the time to make sure that your space is clean, organized, and the best that you can do for this moment in time. It's not about living in a mansion. You can live in a one-bedroom studio apartment. It is what you have for now be content in this space, take care of it, honor it, and know that better is coming as you take care of what you have today. Your restful space is your reward.

A Practical Tool Guide For Prioritizing Your Life

WHAT DID YOU STUDY THIS MONTH?

Make sure that you make a conscious decision to put information into others and into yourself. Study so that you will become the subject matter expert in one area. Put all of your energy in one place and study to become knowledgeable enough to utilize the information and give the experiences you need in a variety of scenarios so that you have the wisdom to implement the information that you have learned.

WHAT DID YOU WATCH ON TV THIS WEEK?

If you watch television, try to utilize your time spent watching TV as a method of renewing and strengthening yourself. It is a moment to tap out of reality and allow your mind to explore, imagine, and remember. Television can be a great tool for helping you to see the world from your home, but do not use it to take you away from activities that would create a better version of your life. While you are watching TV programs that have been created to hold you in place, consider using your time to create something that moves you along.

HOW MANY TIMES DID YOU CHECK SOCIAL MEDIA THIS WEEK? INCLUDING EMAILS DURING OFF WORK HOURS?

Limit the amount of time that you spend in social media activities that do not drive your goals. Social media as an outlet should be used as a limited resource. Scrolling through emails and clicking on social media outlets drain your time from you. Intentionally minimize the amount of time that you give yourself access to your emails and social media even if it is work related. Emails serve as a communication form. Generally, somebody wants something from you. You have enough tasks in front of you currently to work on; go to your emails to hear the communications and what people are requesting from you after your task at hand are completed.

DID YOU SLEEP IN PEACE THIS WEEK?

Your ability to sleep well at night is a gift related to working hard and knowing that you have put the time in. Peaceful nights signify time well spent during the day. People often have a challenge with sleeping through the night if there are open issues pressing on their minds. Unfinished activities, unrealized dreams, incomplete assignments. Spend your day working on one goal at a time to finish things out so that at the end of the day you can reassure yourself that you have completed something with your time. Your brain will rest easier and ask you to accomplish one small thing at a time.

NOW THAT YOU CAN CLEARLY SEE WHERE YOU ARE SPENDING YOUR TIME, MONEY, EFFORTS, AND ENERGY, IS THIS WHERE YOU WANT TO SPEND YOUR LIFE CYCLE?

YOU HAVE A LIMITED AMOUNT OF TIME TO SPEND AS THE PERSON YOU ARE IN THIS LIFE-TIME.

YOU MUST CHOOSE HOW YOU ARE GOING TO INTENTIONALLY SPEND UP YOUR TIME.

We all have been given a measure of time. It is up to us to use it wisely.

"Time is the unit of destiny." - Joshua Selman.

Once your time is use in the wrong way we are taken off the path of true destiny and it takes away from where you are supposed to be at a given time. Each of us has been given a time note that we can use as we choose. Choose wisely because your destiny clock is ticking. You have been given a very specific measure of time to do specific activities so do not allow yourself to get distracted by all the variables of other people's lives. Intentionally reset your activities one moment at a time. When you find yourself going off in the wrong direction, quickly reassess, renavigate, and reassign your activities of choice. Remember, it is always about a choice. We choose everyday and every moment. Time and chance are given to us all it is how we define our priorities and give a measurement of energy to a particular moment. It is true time and change cannot be managed but we are able to get in front our activities and allow the changes that occur to serve us during a given time period. Myles Munroe.

Chapter Ten

The Right Stuff to Get off Your Plate

On a scale from 1 to 10

Question: *How many other people's problems do you have on your plate?*

Success Principle: Learning to say no is a preservative.

Scripture: *Ecclesiastes 3:6, "A time to search and a time to give up, a time to keep and a time to throw away."*

Quote: "Saying no means I care enough to say I cannot give myself fully to this moment" (Dr. Stacy Coward).

CLEAR YOUR PLATE

> Your plate is full. Look at what you can realistically do and give the rest to someone else to eat

Now read this. You may need to restructure your Priority List.

PRIORITY 1 – THEY GET TO SPEAK WITH YOU EVERY DAY. THEY HAVE FULL ACCESS TO YOUR TIME, MONEY, AND RESOURCES. THESE ARE THE PEOPLE YOU ARE DOING EVERYTHING FOR. THEY ARE YOUR END-GAME BENEFICIARIES.

PRIORITY 2 – THEY ARE IMPORTANT TO YOU. HOWEVER, THEY ARE ABLE TO TAKE CARE OF THEMSELVES, AND YOU WANT TO ASSIST THEM TO SECURE THEIR FUTURE AS NEEDED. HOWEVER, YOU ARE ONLY THERE TO ASSIST AS NEEDED. THEY WILL BENEFIT FROM YOUR WORK IN SOME WAY.

PRIORITY 3 – THEY GET THE BENEFITS OF YOUR KNOWLEDGE, EXPERTISE, AND YOU WANT TO MAKE AN IMPACT IN THEIR LIVES ON A MACRO LEVEL. YOU WANT TO HELP THEM TO BECOME THEIR GREATEST VERSION OF THEMSELVES, BUT THEY ARE RESPONSIBLE FOR THEIR OWN LIVES. YOU ARE HERE AS A VOICE FOR THEM OR LEADERSHIP.

PRIORITY 4 AND 5 – THEY ARE TAKING YOUR TIME, MONEY, ENERGY, AND RESOURCES. ELIMINATE THEM FROM YOUR PLATE. GIVE THEM TO SOMEONE ELSE TO ASSIST.

> YOU CANNOT SAVE THE WORLD. CONSIDER THE PEOPLE YOU HAVE IN YOUR TOP THREE PRIORITIES AND PASS THE OTHERS ON TO SOMEONE ELSE.

> You cannot be everything to everyone. It is okay to preserve yourself for yourself and those people who are the priority in your life.

INTENTIONAL STEPS TOWARD YOUR FUTURE

Getting there is more about knowing where you are going versus movement. Many people don't even take the time to think about where they want to actively go. They spend years moving around in spaces and places that they are not even happy in nor even planned to be in. Every ninety days, we should spend our time evaluating our lives and making sure we are intentionally moving in the direction we want to go in.

RELATIONSHIPS THAT COUNT

Many times, we give our life away to the wrong people because we are working in the wrong places and spaces. Living in the here and now with the right people is essential to your growth and continued development. Many people get caught in the same game space and never stop evaluating the people, places, and activities of choice they are spending their life cycle in.

Here are some things to question about your life to make sure you are putting your time, efforts, and energy into the right spaces and places.

On a scale from 1 to 10

____I have great relationships with the people I love the most.

____The people I love the most know how much I love them.

____I am good at showing the people I love how much I love them.

____I can clearly identify who I am responsible for caring for.

____My words and my actions line up in all my significant relationships.

____If I die today, I am satisfied with my relationship.

____I am in the best-case scenario with my partner.

____I am certain that with work, my relationship can be better.

____My activities seen and unseen line up with my words.

____I forgive others quickly.

____I forgive my partner quickly.

____My relationship with my partner is where I want it to be.

____My relationship with my mother is/was good.

____My relationship with my father is /was good.

____My relationship with my siblings is good.

If you want to know what you value, then look at your spending habits. This next exercise will help you to become aware of your spending practices. The goal for making money is to keep the money. If you are spending everything you have, you will never gain the momentum you need to make an impact and reach your goals.

Love yourself and your priorities, number one people, enough to say "no" to anything, robbing you of your profits.

Your spending habits tell it all. Get real with yourself like getting real with your money. If time is money and money is time, then every time you spend money, you spend time. Being a good steward over your money is also being a good steward over your time.

Did you give money to anyone outside of your immediate household/priority 1 people this month? Who? Why?

1. How many times did you eat out?
2. Did you have enough money to meet your personal needs?
3. Was your gas tank full all months?
4. Did you run out of money/food this month?
5. Did you spend money on anything fun this month?
6. Did you give money to the homeless?
7. How much do you spend on groceries?
8. Did you spend money on cigarettes, alcohol, or marijuana this week? How much?
9. Did you save any money this month? How much?
10. Did you ask for a receipt this month and actively look at what you spent?
11. Did you call anyone you owed and tell them when you would pay them?
12. Did you pay for a certification in the past year?
13. How many times did you have to go into any money you saved this month?
14. Did you make a significant effort to correct a past due bill?
15. How many books have you bought in the past year?
16. Did you pay off any past due bills?
17. Do you have an active savings technique daily, weekly,

On a scale from 1 to 10

____I have great relationships with the people I love the most.

____The people I love the most know how much I love them.

____I am good at showing the people I love how much I love them.

____I can clearly identify who I am responsible for caring for.

____My words and my actions line up in all my significant relationships.

____If I die today, I am satisfied with my relationship.

____I am in the best-case scenario with my partner.

____I am certain that with work, my relationship can be better.

____My activities seen and unseen line up with my words.

____I forgive others quickly.

____I forgive my partner quickly.

____My relationship with my partner is where I want it to be.

____My relationship with my mother is/was good.

____My relationship with my father is /was good.

____My relationship with my siblings is good.

If you want to know what you value, then look at your spending habits. This next exercise will help you to become aware of your spending practices. The goal for making money is to keep the money. If you are spending everything you have, you will never gain the momentum you need to make an impact and reach your goals.

Love yourself and your priorities, number one people, enough to say "no" to anything, robbing you of your profits.

Your spending habits tell it all. Get real with yourself like getting real with your money. If time is money and money is time, then every time you spend money, you spend time. Being a good steward over your money is also being a good steward over your time.

Did you give money to anyone outside of your immediate household/priority 1 people this month? Who? Why?

1. How many times did you eat out?
2. Did you have enough money to meet your personal needs?
3. Was your gas tank full all months?
4. Did you run out of money/food this month?
5. Did you spend money on anything fun this month?
6. Did you give money to the homeless?
7. How much do you spend on groceries?
8. Did you spend money on cigarettes, alcohol, or marijuana this week? How much?
9. Did you save any money this month? How much?
10. Did you ask for a receipt this month and actively look at what you spent?
11. Did you call anyone you owed and tell them when you would pay them?
12. Did you pay for a certification in the past year?
13. How many times did you have to go into any money you saved this month?
14. Did you make a significant effort to correct a past due bill?
15. How many books have you bought in the past year?
16. Did you pay off any past due bills?
17. Do you have an active savings technique daily, weekly,

biweekly, monthly?
18. When is the last time you spent money on yourself?
19. Did you make any new bills?
20. Did you buy anything new for your house and it paid off this month?

Look at your priorities by looking at your spending habits. If you do not know where you spent your money, ask for receipts for the next thirty days on everything you spend and sit down weekly to review your habits.

1ST week receipts	2ND week receipts	3RD week receipts	4TH week receipts	5TH week receipts

Is your money going where you want it to go?   YES   or   NO

Here are some things you can consider for money spending as you create a priority list for directing your actions:

Have you identified specific things that you would like to spend your time and effort toward? Think about the next one year, five years, and ten years from now, what will your life look like? We are all forces of energy. It is important for us to have a specific goal in mind to allow our energy to move toward and to guide our thoughts in a direction that helps us to see tangible evidence as result of the use of our energy. Here are just a few ideas on things that may be important to you to invest your time and money buying a house, land, car, vacations, education, or experiences.

Your financial priorities are neither right nor wrong, it is your life, and you get to live it in a way that makes you happy. The goal is to ensure that the activities that you are doing lead you in the direction you want to go into. When you consider your financial priorities, it is merely a snapshot of time that demonstrates what has been important to you during that period of your life cycle. Drive your finances to where you want to go to get to the right spaces, places, and times.

Love yourself enough to guard your inner circle.

It's important to protect yourself by being selective about who you allow in your inner circle. Not everyone should have access to you, as your value increases your vulnerability increases and you must guard how closer you allow people to be around you to speak into your eargate. It's perfectly acceptable to safeguard your most valuable resource, which is yourself. The people you surround yourself with have a direct impact on your thoughts, your emotions, and ultimately, your actions. Your inner circle influences you daily, especially during tough decisions or crises. It's crucial to have someone in your ear who can guide you with intentional movement and encourage you with a deep understanding of who you are.

During life's unpredictable moments, it's helpful to have someone to guide you when you can't see the way forward. This person should be a beacon of light when you feel confused, lost, inexperienced, or unaware. They can also offer spiritual guidance during times of emotional turmoil or financial stress. Your inner circle is crucial, as they know your desires and can help you navigate life's challenges. To protect yourself, be mindful of who you allow into your inner circle, just as you would protect your heart. Your life depends on the people you surround yourself with. Maintaining strong relationships with friends is important. Though it may take effort to renew or reset them, your friends should be aware of what's happening in your life so that you can maintain healthy connections in the present moment. While it's good to reflect on past experiences, it's even better to share stories that are happening in your lives right now so that everyone can be a part of them.

To have fulfilling relationships, it's important to share your personal thoughts and feelings with trusted friends. These individuals should be a part of your inner circle and have the experience and resources to provide valuable feedback. Discussing your plans, fears, concerns, expectations, and goals can help you become a better person and add value to your life. As you grow and evolve over time, your inner circle should also grow and adapt to your changing values. It's important to surround yourself with people who pour into you and empower you to be the best version of yourself.

As you continue to grow, it's important to surround yourself with individuals who support your journey and direction in life. Your inner circle should encourage you to stay focused on your goals while also being present in the moment. You should feel comfortable being yourself around them, knowing that you are loved and respected. Even if you make mistakes, they will honor and support you, giving you the space to learn and grow.

Self-awareness is essential to gaining insight and judgment skills to help you to access your life.

Chapter Eleven

The Right Reason to Keep Going

On a scale from 1 to 10

Question: *Do you know your "WHY"?*

Success Principle: Knowing your WHY is an important variable because it will sustain you when you feel challenged most.

Scripture: *2 Corinthians 4:16–18, "Therefore we do not lose heart. Though outwardly we are wasting away, yet inwardly we are being renewed day by day."*

Quote: "Find your WHY and keep your eyes in that place" (Dr. Stacy Coward).

What's driving your behavior?

Sometimes, we struggle to communicate our desires to others because we may not fully understand what we truly need. It's important to dig deeper and understand the emotions behind our wants. It's not fair to expect others to fulfill our needs if we haven't identified them ourselves. When we become frustrated with others, it's important to recognize that the problem may lie within ourselves. To better understand our emotions and behaviors, we must pinpoint the root cause of our feelings. This can be challenging, but it starts with identifying how we feel, when we feel it, and why we feel that way. This process will help us identify our true needs.

IDENTIFY YOUR WHY

Finish these FOUR SIMPLES statements.

ONLY CHOOSE ONE AT THIS TIME

I FEEL Mad, Sad, Glad, or Afraid.

WHEN does this happen?

BECAUSE "I" STATEMENTS (Write three because statements.)

Now answer what you NEED from yourself first and then from others.

It's crucial to take a moment to reflect on yourself and recognize any areas where you may be struggling. Don't be quick to blame others for your problems. Instead, focus on identifying what changes you can make to improve your life. Often, these changes only require effort from yourself. After reading this book, ask yourself if you have the discipline to continue putting yourself in positive environments, situations, and moments. You have the power to make positive changes in your life, so take control and start making progress today.

Answer this question: Would you stop wrestling a gorilla when they get tired or you get tired?

When considering the importance of being in the right place, at the right time, and with the right people, it's clear that this requires continual self-awareness and discipline. It's important to avoid situations that waste your time and to constantly evaluate your actions and hold yourself accountable to your goals. While this book focuses on surrounding yourself with the right people, ultimately, it's about making the most of your time and living up to your potential. There will always be distractions that can derail you, but it's crucial to stay focused and keep wrestling with the discipline of doing things the right way with the right people at the right time. Don't lose sight of your purpose and keep striving to stay aligned with your goals.

To truly be the best version of yourself every day, it's imperative that you exercise self-discipline and ensure that you remain in the right spaces and places. As you continue to grow, variables will consistently change, so it's essential to stay vigilant about those with whom you have a vested interest. While various scenarios may arise, it's important to recognize that they are merely distractions. It takes discipline to resist the impulse to react, but it's crucial to stay on track. By staying focused and breathing through the urge to respond, you'll remain in control and steadily progress toward your goals.

Chapter Twelve

The Right Answers

On a scale from 1 to 10

Question: *Do you ask the right people the right question?*

Success Principle: Knowing the RIGHT questions to ASK is the BEST way to get the RIGHT answers.

Scripture: *Proverbs 15:23, "A man has joy in an apt answer, And how delightful is a timely word!"*

Quote: "Humility to say I don't know the answers is your superpower" (Dr. Stacy Coward).

Maintaining awareness of your actions and not feeling obligated to answer every question asked of you is crucial. Sometimes, the best decision is to not respond at all. Moreover, it's important to prioritize your own goals and not let other people's emergencies and needs distract you from them. Everyone has their own agenda to fulfill, but you must stay committed to your own path. If you find yourself getting off track, take a moment to reevaluate and realign yourself. Self-awareness is the key to remaining focused on your mission, assignment, and goals. Remember to stay disciplined and not get weighed down by the surrounding noise.

ANSWER: *You stop wrestling when the gorilla gets tired.*

YOU MUST WRESTLE WITH THE GORILLAS IN YOUR LIFE THAT ARE DETERMINED TO TAKE YOU OFF COURSE. YOU HAVE MANY THINGS THAT ARE CONSTANTLY WRESTLING AGAINST YOU TO TAKE YOU OFF YOUR COURSE. FIGHT BACK, WRESTLE, BE SMART, BE INTENTIONAL ABOUT YOUR TIME, EFFORT, AND ENERGY, AND YOU WILL SURELY LAND IN THE RIGHT SPACES, PLACES, AND TIMES.

Question: *When in doubt, what should I do about it?*

Answer: *Mind Your Own Business.*

It's imperative that you prioritize your own well-being and concentrate on improving your quality of life. It's understandable to feel pressure to please others and live up to their expectations, but it's vital to remember that not everyone deserves to be a part of your inner circle. Instead, focus your time and energy on activities that will make you a better person and have a positive impact on those who rely on you. Don't waste your precious time dwelling on past events or worrying about the future. Trust that everything you require is already in place and concentrate on living in the present moment. By doing so, you will be able to fully appreciate and enjoy each moment as it unfolds, without the burden of unnecessary stress and anxiety.

Question: *What if you get distracted?*

Answer: *Keep your eyes on where you are going.*

It seems like you may be struggling with feeling purposeless and unsure of what you are working toward. While you have a general idea of wanting to do well in life, have a good job, and a happy family, it's important to have specific details about your end goal. Trying to figure out all the details between now and the future can be overwhelming and may not be within your area of expertise. However, you don't need to know all the details because God has already ordered your steps. By keeping your focus on your future and trusting that God knows the steps needed to get you there, you can rest assured that everything is okay. God orders our steps and has all the details to our endgame, including the variables and necessary events to make our story line go in the right direction.

Your job is to maintain momentum and direction toward your goal and not lose sight of where you're trying to go. The details of the story can become a distraction, so it's important to keep your focus. Remember, like in the story of Peter walking on water, looking around and getting distracted can cause us to sink. Stay focused on where you're trying to go and trust that the waves, storms, and rain are all necessary parts of the journey to get you to the other side. By keeping your focus and moving in the right direction, you can make progress toward your goals.

Question: *How do I keep track of my time?*

Answer: *Know there are timed seasons.*

It is crucial to understand the different phases of life we go through, which can be compared to seasons. Every season has a beginning and an end, and during each season, we experience growth and development. These various stages of life, from infancy to mature adulthood, require different levels of thinking, behavior, and emotional intelligence. It is essential to recognize which season of life we are in and how we should act accordingly. Additionally, it is crucial to know when a particular season or situation has run its course so that we don't waste our valuable time on something that is no longer relevant. Many people spend their emotional energy and effort on things that no longer serve them, such as dwelling on past relationships or regrets. It is important to acknowledge when it is time to move on and create a new story for ourselves. For instance, if you have finished a race, don't waste time reliving it. Instead, focus on your present and future goals. It is understandable to feel hesitant about starting new things, such as applying for a new job, going on a date, or meeting new friends, especially if one has been hurt before.

However, we should not let our fears hold us back from moving forward and experiencing new things. It is crucial to let go of the past and embrace the opportunities of the present and future.

Question: *What if I get discouraged?*

Answer: *Remember to stay to course.*

You must remember "I AM" responsible for my own future and must fight for it with all my might. Every day is an opportunity for growth and progress toward becoming the best version of myself. I can learn, play, love, forgive, hope, and dream. By focusing on one task at a time, I can see the tangible results of my efforts and be more productive. It's important to avoid distractions, especially fear, which can prevent us from achieving our goals. Instead, we should focus on what we can change and work on improving those areas. Wasting time on negative thoughts or activities that don't serve us is counterproductive. When we find ourselves getting off track, we need to reset our thinking and focus on what inspires us to keep going. Self-awareness is key to staying on course. We need to be mindful of our emotions and behaviors and align them with positive thinking. Having a go-to scripture, quote, or motivational saying can help us reset our thinking in challenging moments. Distractions are always present, but we must not let them stop us. We must decide to keep moving forward, even when it's tough. We can rethink, renegotiate, revamp, or restart, but we must not give up. Our time is valuable, and we have already invested so much into our goals. We owe it to ourselves to finish what we started.

As you reflect on these thoughts, remember that we only have one chance to seize once-in-a-lifetime opportunities. Therefore, your time is one of your most essential resources as you consider how to spend your life. Think about the people who are fortunate enough to have you in their lives. You are an asset. Some people want to be part of your inner circle because of the value you bring to their lives. Your mere presence is a gift. I understand that this may sound conceited, arrogant, or even entitled. However, the truth is that all your life experiences have shaped you into a complex human being who continues to evolve, and there is no definitive answer to who you are. Your life is intricate, with many twists and turns that create dynamics that make you exceptional. Given all the struggles, challenges, and obstacles you have faced and overcome, it would be a shame to waste your life on the wrong person. Loving yourself is an art, and you deserve to give yourself and your top priority people the best part of your life. Always remember that you are a priority. Enjoy your journey as you learn and cultivate the art of self-love.

PS. *My time was well spent with you for these moments it took for you to complete this book.*

www.ingramcontent.com/pod-product-compliance
Lightning Source LLC
LaVergne TN
LVHW041542060526
838200LV00037B/1101